Freya Manfred | *Loon In Late November Water*

BY FREYA MANFRED

POETRY

A Goldenrod Will Grow
Yellow Squash Woman
American Roads
Flesh And Blood
My Only Home
The Blue Dress
Swimming With A Hundred Year Old Snapping Turtle
Speak Mother

MEMOIR

Frederick Manfred: A Daughter Remembers
Raising Twins: A True Life Adventure

Freya Manfred

LOON IN LATE NOVEMBER WATER

Red Dragonfly Press

ISBN 978-1-945063-23-7 paper

Library of Congress Control Number: 2018956355

Acknowledgments: "On Carpinteria Beach" and "Many Things Frighten Me" were published in 2018 by *Poets Speak Anthology.*

Cover photo by Bly Pope
Author portrait: "My mother, Freya Manfred" pencil drawing
    by Bly Pope

Designed and typeset by Scott King
    using Warnock Pro (text) & Centaur Pro (titles)

Published by Red Dragonfly Press
    P. O. Box 98
    Northfield, MN 55057
    www.reddragonflypress.org

Contents

The revisions of these poems were guided by the loving and perceptive suggestions of my husband, Thomas Pope, and our sons, Nicholas Bly Pope and Ethan Rowan Pope, and the support of the brilliant Scott King, publisher. My heartfelt thanks to these four good men—how can I ever repay them?

Pass The Kolaches

I tell my mother that my old friend loved the poem I wrote for his wife's funeral. Mother passes me a plate of poppy seed Kolaches, and says, "You've had a successful life. You're of help to someone." Mom is eighty-nine, and often says that she's "no use to anyone anymore," and that it's "ridiculous" her life has come to its near-end so suddenly. "The whole thing is incomprehensible," she mutters. "Unbelievable. Where did it all go?" She's not sad, depressed, or even angry. It's some other emotion: perhaps a down-to-earth Slovak, trying to make sense of the universe.

Every time I finish a poem, I feel as if I'm nearing the end of my life, but that I'm not old, young, furious, or loving enough to have anything to offer with all my pages full of words.

Poems written by myriads of writers flow out in books, the Internet, the airwaves, in bars, on stage, even on the screen. Am I supposed to comprehend, love, or even like all these poems? I don't. Am I supposed to care what illusions or allusions, what famous or never-heard-of signature follows each careful, laborious, love-infused phrase? I don't.

I can't remember a lot of what I read or hear. I barely recognize my own name at the end of my inky, heartfelt cries. Here I am, yes here I am! Here you are, yes here you are! Are we writers helping anyone gain back their voting rights? Can we install a window or fix a washing machine? Who will watch our children's children if we're up in the attic in a January blizzard, flushed with uncommon intensity, scribbling on each other's scribbles, begging for attention, and trying to bring home a little bread?

When I taught a poetry class at the University, one middle-aged male student told me on the last day of class that I'd been no help to him at all, and worse, I'd wrecked the class "entirely" for him by "allowing some sick young woman to babble on and on about menstruation."

"That was the topic of her poem," I said.

"That word shouldn't be allowed in any poem, or spoken aloud in any good class on poetry! Too violent, vivid, and insensitive—not what we want or need to hear about!"

"But, Mr. Z, you wrote and read a very fine violent and vivid poem about the bloated, grotesquely mutilated body you and your buddies found off a dock in the Hudson River."

"I don't see the comparison!" he yelped.

After I waved goodbye to him, I turned out the classroom lights for the last time and stood in the darkness. Suddenly, the lights flicked on again, and three of my students came in, smiling. One of them, a man from China who was studying to become a doctor, handed me a bouquet of flowers. "Thanks for helping me live in two worlds at once," he said.

"And sometimes three," said the second student. "For understanding that I'm Native American, American, and human!" This young man's grief-filled poems were also heart-rendingly funny, a miracle few writers achieve.

After the third student, a shy woman from a small town, hugged me and whispered her goodbye, I found my way to the car and drove home in a blizzard of tears.

I have no idea what I can tell my mother as she nears the end. She's done a great deal for others, with her marvelous, eager brain, peering through what she often saw as life's long dark tunnel. As a girl I had a hard time when she felt depressed, but I also told stories and laughed with her. She stroked my forehead when I had the flu, and I held her hand when she was sick in the hospital.

Like her, I can't believe life has gone by so fast. It's all come down to this? All that poetry?! No one can be a perfect poet, teacher, daughter, or mother. And no one should have to pretend to be any of them. If I love your poems, I'll tell you. If not, please pass the Kolaches.

These Poems

These poems are born from my dreams,
who come like gentle friends every night,
dab wet hands on my forehead,
sway in my breath.

The dreams don't know
I flatten them on these pages, into poems.
Perhaps they won't like it.

They don't know I throw them to my poem animal
who molds them with his claws,
licks them clean, and eats them.

I want to give you
the gentle dream friends and the poem animal.
I write these poems
so I won't have to explain what they mean,
or how they came to be.

I

LOON IN LATE NOVEMBER WATER

Even if it's all done in a secret loneliness, the true work
won't fail us.
– James Wright, *A Wild Perfection*

When The Lake Wakes Me

I open my eyes and the eye of the lake is waiting,
wide and deep,
filled with silver ripples that lead me home.

After a long night,
the lake sends its borrowed sun and shadow
back into me once more.

I love to swim with swarming sun fish
and often think of them as friends.
If I'm lucky, they'll wonder who I am today.

Eyes wide, we weave through lilies,
swallowing bits of reed and weed
like mother's milk—

all of us, together, devoured and devouring,
in this age-old water,
singing a fierce wordless song of being here, alive.

Loon In Late November Water

A loon throws up her wings,
then dives and disappears,
then surfaces again, almost beyond my sight.

I can't see her blood-red eyes,
but she's as white as the new-falling snow
and as black as the branches of the barren trees.

She swims so long and far beneath the waves
that I can't recall where she vanished
or guess when or where she might rise again.

This is how writing poetry feels to me.

Some determined creature plunges underwater,
then rises to the surface,
then drops down deep, again—
a motion the animal in me embraces—
exploring rich, half-remembered places,
and then a bold resurfacing.

Now, as cold takes over the land
and the sky grows both lovely and dangerous,
I try to live like the loon, on the surface and below,
visible, then invisible, even to myself.
And this journey continues every living, dying moment
until the loon flies south for the winter.

But I never wait to watch her fly away.

The Loon Speaks

The loon speaks in tones that rise from a watery place,
like the sounds we hear in the womb
echoing the ancient sharks of the soul,
those eternal cries of quickening joy and sorrow.

Loons aren't as friendly as dolphins, and won't be trained.
They ride the waves like stern grandfathers and grandmothers,
heads high, beaks thrust forward,
blood-red eyes reflecting our bloody birth.

Loon is beyond anything except *loon*.
If you see one, you haven't met one.
Sometimes I wonder if they're even from this planet,
perhaps because they were here long before us
and plan to stay long after we're gone.

That's what they cry: *Here! Here I am. Here! Here I am.*

Wonder And Joy

Joy is yellow, and melts into amber, maize, or gold.
But wonder can be many colors: green, indigo, ebony, or rose.
The last time I felt joy melt in my mouth, past thought or doubt,
was yesterday, when our two tall sons bent to hug me.
But I feel wonder all the time. Everything's a surprise:
his words, her song, the wrong turn, a false friend, a good neighbor,
all so startling and new, even when ancient or anticipated.

Joy always leads to wonder, but wonder doesn't always lead to joy.
Wonder can also lead to sorrow, rage, or death.
Joy flies in, with its own free will, but wonder is in every wave.
And the wonder of wonder is that I never know what to do about it,
good or bad, so I celebrate the human toll we sometimes pay for it.

You might suspect I'm depressed if I say I rarely feel joy
or that I'd like more of it in my life, but I'm truly grateful,
dreaming or meditating right here, embraced by wonder.

Maybe we discover joy—or inhabit wonder—most deeply
when we make love, or when we're dying.
Yet our children often move more flawlessly or gracefully
toward joy and wonder than we do.
Joy and wonder travel everywhere with them,
and emanate utterly, and unutterably, from them. At every turn.

Who We Are When We Don't Know Who We Are

The more you say you don't know who you are,
the more I know you are.

Part rock, part river, part tree.
Part roots of grass, seeking beyond you and me.
Part earth, sky, and raging sea.

Part yolk and part shell.
Part moon's scars and sun's burnt glory.
Part word, part page, and part book.

Part inner space and part outer space.
Part first breath, and last.
Part you, and me, and all of us, moving as one.

But call out the names of everyone and every thing
and there will always be one thread, one fiber,
that is forever you—

a flavor, or color, a tick of the tock,
often unseen or unheard,
a single musical note, a song and a summons.

The Long-Grassed Hair Of God

> Who can see the green earth anymore
> as she was by the sources of Time?
> – Matthew Arnold

In my shy and solitary childhood tadpoles and minnows
swam beside me in a swift silver dream,
rabbits taught me to hop, then wait, mute, under the bushes.

Squirrels led me up trees, where the leaves were full of songs,
and orioles summoned me into the sky
until one blossoming June day—I flew over our plum tree!

All these new friends sang or spoke a simple wondrous prayer
in a vast green, blue, brown, black, and white church
where I found no end of adventure and repose,

despite bumps, scrapes, or large and small murders—
as we all wisely, cunningly, desperately,
tried to survive each holy and uncharted day and night.

Soon I sang my own small hymns on the highest hill,
my fingers combing the long-grassed hair of God,
while I dared to wonder who or what I would become.

Intent on the myriad, mystifying messages and voices,
I learned to see with a fox's eyes as well as a frog's—
a girl's eyes as well as a boy's.

Each of us has waited a long time to see each other,
and learn from each other, and know each other,
and praise each other, in the eternal book of earth.

Old Friends

Old friends are a steady spring rain,
or late summer sunshine edging into fall,
or frosted leaves along a snowy path—
a voice for all seasons saying, *I know you.*
The older I grow, the more I fear I'll lose my old friends,
as if too many years have scrolled by
since the day we sprang forth, seeking each other.

Old friend, I knew you before we met.
I saw you at the window of my soul—
I heard you in the steady millstone of my heart
grinding grain for our daily bread.
You are sedimentary, rock-solid cousin earth,
where I stand firmly, astonished by your grace and truth.
And gratitude comes to me and says:

"Tell me anything, and I will listen.
Ask me anything, and I will answer you."

"Get It Together," You Say

How do I do that? How do *you* do it?
Who says I have the power to see my life whole?

I see the radiant face of a four year old on a swing,
the scent of lilacs and peonies, tea parties with stuffed animals,

a handmade wooden sled slicing down a long white hill,
a lovely mother in a lavender coat, a proud father, at work and play.

I see an ethereal little sister, a plucky baby brother,
and a Slovak grandmother, grateful to be our warm lap.

And years later, I see the bewilderment of brains and bodies
depleted by age, pain, sweat, shock, and fate.

And balancing this, I see two bright children, love and gladness
in one lucky, unforgettable birth.

I admire the young ones' better nature, their secret inner calm,
righteous anxiety, overflowing humor, and hard work.

Here is the family and all their creations—that outpouring
of laughter. Those tears from the gods.

These dear faces flow together, in bookstores, on horseback,
starting the Ford, cutting down the Christmas tree,

petting the dog, dancing in the dark, reading by the fire,
at breakfast, at dinner, under the stairs, and beyond the stars...

...and on we go, and on. Where? How? For how long?
Everything and everyone swept by the tides of what will be.

Beyond a gigantic puzzle or a great mystery, beyond dreams
or storybooks, work or play, I ask:

What freedom was born? What knowledge came freely?
Who would we be, if we were more truly free?

Does anyone grasp life entirely at the moment of living it?

I sit here, two feet on the table, an apple in one hand,
and an old friend steps into the room.

Suddenly, I have it "together." A friend just stepped into my room.

Sleeping In The Poet's Studio

It's been years since I spent all night awake
in a room above the city rooftops

where giant oaks weighted with white stars and snow
reach halfway to the moon,

where not sleeping is life's blood,
because the poet whose rooms I wander has traveled away,

leaving behind gnomic words and phrases on torn pages,
stuffed into books, or scattered free,

words so moving, so classic and engaging,
I decided to write a few lines myself in the pale dark.

But soon I stopped writing my poem
and summoned a prayer for all poets instead,

an old song, of time and chance, long life and good health,
which I can't sing or say to you,

because I'm more friendly oak and silent moon
than poet, now.

For Robert and Ruth Bly

Fear Of Literary Parties

I stop before I enter a roomful of writers,
as the animal inside me cries, "Get away,
before it's too late!" Towering there,
whiskey in hand, is the world-famous
raconteur, who wants every other writer
at the bar to fail. Stalwart in his shadow,
sipping wine, is the sly critic, who says
poems and fiction should never tell a story.
Behind him, martini-eyed, his fourth wife
wonders if anyone remembers that she's
a writer, too. Gliding among them, a-chitter,
is the wildly successful poet, tolling a long,
cerebral thesis no one dares to interrupt.
And this scenario continues while I escape
to the moonlit porch to settle my heart,
and gaze, brooding, at the diamond-white
glimmer of Los Angeles, the lilac-scented
Minneapolis lakes, the untamed canyons
of Manhattan—until an old woman poet
standing beside me says, "You're still young,
still strong. A true poet. Good as any.
So come, devour my blue-veined stories.
Ripe with what I sing, you'll become richer
than you were before you arrived.
We'll be conspirators outside the circle
of caws and coos—monstrous in our need
for words from the blessed un-dead,
the sacred long dead, and ourselves—
and all the other hard-writing human liars."

To My Mentors

I don't want to leave you
but in some way I don't understand
I leave everyone
when I follow the voice
rising in me,
the voice I found beside the lake,
the voice I didn't know was mine.

How can I miss you so much and yet speak
with the truest, most certain voice
I've had in years?
You said the voice was there long ago,
but I do not think I heard it speak.
(As far as I know
you've never seen a word I've written.)

Even as I talk with you now
I can't believe the joy I feel because I'm the one
speaking calmly, not frightened or alone.
If I can keep the sound of water
rippling steadily inside me
I will have swallowed
what I need to make it to my end.

Peace At The Lake

In the rare morning hour
when maple leaves and pine needles are still,
and the windless lake lies motionless
under a skein of silver threads,
no eagle cries, and no boat throbs upon the water.

Silent sunlight replaces the fog
that vanishes into each rock and grass blade.
Sap flows, soundless, through trees, flowers, clouds,
and even my juice-filled brain,
and nothing dies that is part of the whole.

Peace is a motionless faith in motionless silence
that reminds me not to worry, wish, or think,
but to grow in hope with the earth,
with Leaf, Wood, Stone, Fog, Flowers,
Blood, Bone, and Light—
not a blind or unblemished faith—
but changing
when the rains come and the lake weeps,
and laughter rises on the wind.

Dream Lake

This is my dream lake.

When it's calm and sunny, clouds float on the water
until the wind rises—and the wind always rises—
full of leaves, raging with rain or snow.

I sit on shore for hours with my arms around myself
while the dream lake holds me in its sway.
Soft or loud, the sound of waves never leaves me.

You may think I'm asleep, or lost, but even when the lake
is frozen indigo, the water beneath is ready, throbbing,
with thin, thick, broken, unbreakable skin.

This is who I am and will always be—
a naked voice, surrounded by continents.

II

NIGHT IS THE TIME OF RECKONING

In our dreams—I know it!—we do make the journeys we seem to make; we do see the things we seem to see; the people, the horses, the cats...are real, not chimeras; they are living spirits, not shadows; and they are immortal and indestructible.

— Mark Twain, "My Platonic Sweetheart"

Forgive Me, Brother

All night I paged through books of poems
by friends, by enemies, by eastern poets and western poets,
and I could not find one poem that says how I feel,

a poem so sad that my body could collapse into it,
the way stars race into black holes and are gone forever—
a poem which would also hand me one flower.

I couldn't find the right poem for my brother, who is dying,
and for my heart, which grows more insane with joy and longing
each moment I'm still alive.

I couldn't even find a pen to write my own poem.
And when I did find a pen, the cat came to purr on my chest,
and I threw her out with such vengeance!

Now, perhaps, I can forgive myself my life.

To My Brother

How well you hide your fear of dying
with your quick wit, laughter, and concern for detail:
wind speed, temperature, chance of snow,
arrival and departure dates, and who will drive
now that you no longer trust yourself to travel alone.

At times your family surrounds you,
though you schedule many days away from them,
saying you need solitude to ease what cannot mend.
Your illness surrounds you with rumor, innuendo,
pity, concern, and offerings to gods you know are mute.

Rare good friends and passionate strangers
penetrate the sweet, solemn fog of flowers and food,
while others remember becoming ill, like you,
and stay away for fear of disintegrating, painfully,
against their wish or will.

But those who know you for more than your illness,
find you in the light of your eyes,
that green sea of your self, your last energy and love.
Delighted to love you, these wise ones
do not bask in your eventual end, but in you.

Honor

I'm honored to stroke your face, brother,
honored to urge you to sleep, and dream an amazing dream,
honored to be alive when you are dying,
and to embrace your dying,
to embrace your grace while it lingers here,
where no one knows who you are now,
if they ever did—you lonely one,
almost as lonely as I am,
stroking your face to tell you,
"Sleep, rest, dream your best dream...
of being lucky to live for so long."
Your great staring eyes face us, shadows to you now,
shadows of what we were, of what you were,
shadows waiting on your shadow.

His Face After Death

Tears are my constant anchors to time and place,
along with holding hands, the meadow lark's song,
the voice of a man who still loves me,
and the voice of a woman equal to my pain.
But my dead brother's face is no anchor.

Here is the oldest, coldest grimace in the world,
a void that strips sensation and emotion,
a look that travels back into itself,
even into the past that flowed before his birth
and will flow after his death.

Nor is the tick tock of my clock an anchor,
or the forever freeway of ghosts who rush to greet me
when I'm alone, the dead who pass by reminding me
of my last clear memory of my brother's face:
all nothing and nothingness.

Night Is The Time Of Reckoning

Three months after he died
I felt my brother lying next to me,

yes, close beside me, his warm body
against my right arm and leg.

I didn't speak. Neither did he.
It wasn't a time for talk.

It was enough that he came—arrived—
in what you might call a dream

but I call it everyday life.

I felt no fear, no anger or surprise,
and for once no sense of loss—

for myself, or for him—
just a quiet peace for us both,

a simple sister, a simple brother,
who once knew and still know each other,

lying silent, safe, and alive.

Don't Take Me With You

Father died, but he didn't take me with him,
not even down the long corridor I sometimes visit
when we talk about the river or the stars.
Mother died, too. Of course she didn't take me with her,
because I wouldn't have gone. Even as a child
I could see she was used to being deserted, beautifully alone,
like me, when someone I love walks out the door.

My brother died fighting to get back home in May,
his favorite month. I didn't go with him, either.
In a dead white room he hurt, he bled, he begged for help
when there was nothing the living or dead could do.
Instead, his dreaming brain crushed grapes for wine,
rescued a mistreated woman,
and traveled across continents with longtime friends.

Perhaps I could have taken these dear ones by the hand
and journeyed with them, as a daughter, sister, or friend.
But death didn't take me, too. So here I am.
I tell myself they are not far away,
and yet I refuse to join them.
Yes, I cast them out and away—breathe them away
with every breath—each morning as I rise.

What's Always True

Sometimes I predict things that aren't yet true,
but then they happen.

I cherish my own accidental power,
but I hope no one else has the same magic.

I can't bear to hear what others foretell
about me or those I love.

Besides, my predictions are only a possibility,
my last chance to feel free—

to walk an imaginary path to a secret lake,
where I find time to sleep, to dream,

to wonder at a world so new, so very old,
and all I have until I die—

until I die, and the earth goes on turning
for another four billion years—

until I die—which is the one prediction
that always comes true.

Who Will Help Me Die?

Who will help me when I'm dying,
trapped in bed, or on some mindless battlefield?

Let it not be in a windowless nursing home
asking a stranger who I am.

Who will hold my hand while my breath grows
shallow, more shallow, even more shallow?

Doctors won't say how long I have to live.
They've been fooled by death too many times.

Nurses may say I'm waiting for my family to leave
so I can die in peace, but I don't want them to leave!

I hope someone will say whatever helps.
"She wants to know when to let go."

"She hears everything you say, even as she sleeps."
"If you hold her hand, she'll know you're here."

"If you hold her head in your hands,
and put your face above hers, it will calm her."

But who will say these words for me?

The White House Requests The Pleasure Of Your Company

When you wrote, friends and fellow poets,
asking me to submit a poem or statement of conscience
for a reconstituted Poets Against the War movement,
I was not at home with the deep-diving loons of Minnesota,
or anywhere near the iron range lakes and forests I love.
My husband and I were in the chemical outback of New Jersey,
cleaning toilets and cooking soup made with a stock of old steak bones
for my father-in-law, a decorated Colonel in the Philippines,
World War II—who recalls those battles and his men
as clearly now as he remembers his own family,
and often says that war was the formative experience of his life.
He's eighty-six, and bent. But I submit that when I asked him
how he felt about the President's proposed attack on Iraq, he said,
lifting his proud hawk nose over the steam of the soup,
the kitchen light deepening the scar on his forehead,
"If you think we were not always afraid, you're wrong.
If you think we didn't watch out for each other, think again.
We had half the world behind us, and it was not enough."

On Carpinteria Beach

On Carpinteria beach where the Chumash lived for 10,000 years,
saltwater washes across shells and seaweed,
erasing tiny air holes where mussels breathe and wait,
and rivulets of black pitch once used to make canoes
ooze from ancient pits along the shore.
Ten years after Spanish ships arrived with long guns and smallpox
a few Chumash were left alive, while thousands
lay buried in the Mission, bone on bone.

Now, laughing dogs chase seagulls across the sand,
and surfers in slick wetsuits park their pick-up trucks
and trot barefoot into the rising waves,
while scientists from the university peer into tide pools,
jotting notes and muttering,
and white-haired men and women in tennis shoes and floppy hats
slow-step, arm in arm,
or stop to watch the setting sun strike silver from the sea.

And down the coast past the train tracks,
sea lions lie like slabs of lard, waiting to give birth,
or wallow into the water to cool off, weightless as butterflies.
And all day and night the sea curls toward land
and smashes, smashes, smashes—
and says *nothing lasts forever...*

Letter From California

> For my student, Mike Her Many Horses, who left two ducks from
> his hunt on my kitchen table, and departed without a word.

In California the King's Highway is hemmed in by fire hydrants,
   paper cups, parking lot lamps, and long, low, beige buildings.
   Buildings not as sweet and firm as a blade of crabgrass with its
   mesh and liquid green fill. Buildings that might collapse any
   minute, constructed with pizza crust, dog shit, coke straws,
   dollar bills, pie tins, hot dog buns, newspapers, and a farty, ex-
   haust-piped wind.

Cars flow everywhere, mingling and mangling. They have their own
   minds and are bent on going their own way. They careen along
   winding roads to the ocean cliffs and leap into the water, grind-
   ing into the rocks and cutting off the heads of seals and otters
   with one swipe of their open trunks.

I walk the sidewalk with gum on my sandals and hold my breasts
   high to avoid the crowds. I am briefly delighted with the snaky
   slithy posture of the girl with long blonde hair who strokes her
   boyfriend's ass, gives him a goodbye pat, and jumps into the bus.
   Inside, leaning against my left arm, she tells me with a round,
   pink, smoke-puffing mouth that her sister died from a heroin
   overdose two years ago. She hands me some Vitamin E and B
   enriched health food bread; it tastes good. Her name is Melody;
   she has a three-year-old daughter; she works as a topless danger.
   She's a little high now; she has courage, but weed gives her more.

I hitchhike through Oakland. The driver of a Volkswagon Bus calls
   Australia on his cell phone while speeding down Freeway 101
   eating a foot long hot dog.

I am open-mouthed. I run from city cluster to city cluster along the
King's Highway getting a headache and a wobbly heart and hope-
lessly grinning.

Under a freeway bridge during a moment when no cars are passing,
a miracle:

I think of your silence, under a deep-rooted cottonwood tree by the
Missouri River.
I think of the stillness of your arms crossed over your long body and
your legs crossed on the grass.
I think of the cool, hushed caves in the undersides of the mushrooms
growing by your narrow foot.
I think of the silver-white wood of the cottonwood branches under
those wide-spaced Dakota clouds.
I think of worms making delicate tunnels in the silver splinters.
I think of your quiet hands with veins branching in them stroking the
silver wood with wandering finger tips in the prickling silence of
evening.
I dissolve in the river veins, the wood veins, and the veins of your
hands.
You are with me, friend, when I step out to be buried on the King's
Highway.

California Christmas

Seven skinny Santas stroll the beach
with a dozen drunken elves in short red pants.

White egrets stand like oracles in the salt marsh.
Golden bulbs and silver wreathes shimmer in the oleanders.

Surf boards loom like relics, signposts in the sand.
Dark dorsal fins divide the highest waves.

Sullen teenagers in black clothes smoke cigarettes
and cling to the rocks, cawing.

Dogs bark. Children scream. Adults sip beer. A tiny girl
devours a slice of pink-frosted cake as big as her head.

Everyone smiles in the supermarket,
clinking the wine bottles and pinching the roasted chicken.

The next day they all look so crabby.
But how can they feel sad in California at Christmas?

Look at that blue island out there, waiting.
Feel that sun!

The Writer At Heaven's Gate

So I'm walking up and down in front of heaven's gate
talking aloud to myself, as usual,
and people show up, hoping to get in.
"Where am I?" they ask, or, "Lord, what happened?"
And they tell me everything:
the bills they couldn't pay,
the flowers and candy they stole,
the mother they rarely invited to dinner,
the father who promised to help, but wouldn't,
the children they couldn't feed, or fed too much,
the sisters or brothers who died on battlefields
or drowned in undeserved despair.
They tell me as many glorious and gory details
as there are dust motes in the sky.
Sometimes what they say opens the gates,
when even the angels didn't think they'd get in,
and sometimes what they tell me sends them to hell
faster than any devil could dream.
I have no power over this:
I'm the stenographer, the faithful secretary,
the odd, helpless old hermit in the corner who listens,
weeping and worrying after they've gone on,
either direction: they all go *somewhere*.
But for me it's not any different than it was on earth,
the same as if I were never born, as if I never died.

Grateful

I should be grateful to have lived this long,
laughing and talking with my family around our table.

But I'm not sure what grateful *is*.

Maybe it's the feeling that surrounds and protects me
when I leave the grocery with a bag of potatoes,

or when an old friend brushes a gray hair from my cheek
while I tell him my greatest sorrow,

or when I no longer feast upon my deepest fears,
or notice my age, my name, or how I came to be,

and I'm so at peace I don't expect my heart to rupture
or imagine the plane will explode.

But sometimes gratitude ebbs away like water in sand.

Maybe grateful is living every day as if I'm about to die.

III

HEART WORK

The work of the eyes is done. Go now and do the heart-work
on the images imprisoned within you.
– Rainer Maria Rilke

Many Things Frighten Me

Many things frighten me as I age,
especially people with serious illnesses,
but I can't tell them I worry,
for fear they'll feel insulted.
They're more than their pain or crutches,
but I'm not reassured.
I'm still a girl waiting for my wheezing father
to rise from his sickbed,
where he fights another flu or cold
that could kill him.
I always feared the end of dad
would be the end of me.
Mom had tuberculosis, too,
and gasped for breath
when she tried to run or play with me.
They tried to keep their fears a secret
because Dad said I was too sensitive
and Mom said it was my siblings
who couldn't bear the misery of this world;
but the germs they told us about
invaded the house each winter,
dropping with the freezing snow,
festering in the rutted country roads,
sucking the color from their cheeks.
They needed comfort, more than I could give.
Flailing, whispering, shouting,
they tried to stay calm, and failed,
then tried again, linked by the fear
of watching others die, of dying themselves,
of losing us, and earth, this precious place,
this priceless battleground.

Baseball

I strode away into the wild woods and fields
while my father and brother leaped to their feet
in front of the TV, cheering for the Cubs or the Twins.
Years later, I've dived in, too, and at last, I get it—
the peace that descends when I scan the green,
fan-shaped field, the determined faces of the divine,
wiry men, their wide eyes, muscular wrists,
elastic elbows, and the endless sky above—waiting.
Baseball is geometry gone rogue, with rebels
and mavericks in the mix. It's predictable
unpredictability, sometimes a failing rhythm,
sometimes a win. It's start and stop, ebb and flow,
chewing and spitting, signals and mitt slaps—
then pitch, swing, hit, and run! Baseball is war:
smoke signals and secret signs, high diplomacy
and riotous espionage, plots and counterplots
in cloak-and-dagger dugouts. And those long
humbling pauses between pitches are like the deep,
mysterious silences between the words in a good poem.

For Frederick and his Cubs, Frederick Junior and his Twins.

Fancy Killer Car

One dark night I sat in our car and suddenly realized its power.
It seemed alien, as if borrowed from outer space,
rock-hard silver and steel, only recently adopted by us earth worms.
I saw that it could snap tendons, strip skin, and crush bone,
turn my brain to jellyfish, dead and stinking on the shore.
It possessed amazing speed, force, and distance,
an endless marvel: with no heart, no soft landing,
and no safe haven like a lover's arms.

I saw no smile or grin on its grid, not even a grimace,
no sense of rocking in water like a boat,
or trusting to wings and feathers like a bird—
just a clever, herculean way to save time, get anywhere, chop-chop—
leave my old life behind for the space-devouring star travel
we all supposedly long to experience.

And I saw that I was an animal with a short life span
on a great blue-green planet soaring through time and space,
and the other planets and stars were all the eyes of gods—
and I became too smart, too humble, too human—
to start my dangerous, scary, utterly, unutterably formidable
fancy killer car—and drive away.

Girl, With Buckets

How many buckets full to the brim
can the young girl carry to the orchard?
Apples and pears await her in the hot summer night,
so she pours carefully, arms rigid with the weight,
and trudges back to the pump for more.

All the fruit trees must be fed before dark
because trees need well water if there's no rain.
Her bull-shouldered father usually carries the buckets,
but she must have misbehaved or failed some duty,
and this is her punishment.

As clouds fade in the last light of the setting sun
the girl flounders to and fro, to and fro—
keeping faith that all will be well, at last,
if only she can deliver the precious water
to the tender, yearning roots, branches, and fruit.

Time passes vividly into breath and blood,
and for the rest of her life the girl with buckets
will try to succor and sustain her family, past or present.
She will dream that every task and harvest
can be shared equally in this toiling world
where she grew up learning her lesson well.

But some day the woman she will become
will put her burden down.

Mushroom Mother

I snuggle under the quilt with my beautiful, sorrowful mother
to read *Alice in Wonderland*, and we're bourne away
from cooking or cleaning into mushroom make-believe
with the wise and cranky Caterpillar, who cries,
"One side will make you grow taller,
and the other side will make you grow shorter."

Later, the pock-marked morels we find by the river
make Mom smile. "We'll sauté them in butter!"
Grandma rocks on her painful, poorly-mended legs
and picks apron-fulls for our scrambled eggs.
Dad isn't sure they're safe to eat, but we women gobble
and smack our fat mushroom lips.

Years later, Mom is betrayed by a deadly mushroom
that looks like those she picked and ate for years—
but an antidote is found to save her life—
and now she sits smiling across from me,
her skin a smooth, soft mushroom brown,
wrinkled in places like a woodland mushroom.

Her white cap of hair and ears are rounded mushrooms, too.
She's a real mushroom woman with deep roots in the dark earth!
And don't forget her everlasting gray eyes, rain-swollen heart,
and all her powerful, potent, sometimes poisonous,
forever loving and life-giving ways.

Dread

Dread calls at dawn or midnight
from new and ancient times.
It looms like a wolfish winter over the land.

Dread is a lie.
Something lurks beneath it,
the way rage seethes under pride.

Beneath my dread
is a weary soul afraid of greater weariness,
afraid of a future in league with a fearful past.

When dread's rotten breath fills the house,
I try to knock it down with my fist,
or bury it in my trembling heart—

and then, at last, I fall down, and weep,
and all the dead shadows
disappear.

The Fearful Ones

It's a long and rotting road we take,
when, too young to understand,
we learn to fear the deep-thundering remark,
the shove or kick made by a sick, lost mind,
the blows struck without thought
that leave us flailed, broken, crucified and buried.
And we can't all rise from the dead, you know.
Even God deserts some of us.

The perfect parents with their gorgeous certainty,
heads swollen larger than their shadows—
they know how we should, and will, by God, behave!
So we children, bleating and mourning,
stumble through the backwoods as best we can,
with downhill slog and uphill slog,
and no one—ever—gets a breather.

The answer? Creep toward the fearful ones,
until we disappear into their brains
and discover a place we won't dare to visit again.
Or turn and walk away until we're invisible,
free to live and die where our hearts beat easy
and a greater good is promised every day.
And if they ring or knock, we won't reply.
We won't say why. You've done your share.

And so have I.

Walking On Eggshells

> Remember that every life is a special problem which is
> not yours but another's, and content yourself with the
> terrible algebra of your own.
> – Henry James, *Letters*

Careful what you do or say, or they'll slam the door in your face.
You've crossed some line where pain and madness rule.

Anything could happen. They'll leap in front of a truck,
fall from a bridge, plunge a knife to their heart or glass to their wrist.

Or the show could go on forever, a play you'll never exit,
until you feel so numb you fear you'll become a stone.

You have no power to change anyone, so there's no escape
from the bottom of this sea, and no navy to rescue you.

But one way out is to accept that you'll always care.
You just refuse to wait for the next sneak attack. So let go!

And when they die, will you visit their grave?
After you visit the graves of those who were tender and kind? No.

No one can make you their savior or mourner, except you.
And you've swallowed enough guilt—and lasting sorrow.

Understanding The Lost Soul

What does understanding mean? To stand under?
                              To bear the weight?

Maybe the raw truth of the burden you carry
is that you grew up in a frenzied maelstrom of lost promises,
                              and unstaunched wounds.
But I can no longer wade into the horror of it
over years or decades,
                              oh dear, frightened, desperate
                              abuser!

                    Somewhere
        a blue flower opens amid tall prairie grasses,
                    a hawk floats,
        a faint wind blows toward you, past you, into the future,
                    and that peaceful place,
                which belongs to no one and everyone,
        will surround you and soothe you,
                    even if no one whispers your name.

                Here, you can comfort yourself.

I can't placate your flayed nerves any longer,
                won't open my door again to drunken ghosts
                who say "goodbye!"
                              when "hello" beckons.

Don't tell me you've given up on friends and family
                because one day someone did not
                              or could not
                permit you to do exactly what you wished
                or give you exactly what you wanted.

Little girl!—little boy!—
little soul—
we were all children!
We were all needy, and lost hope.
We could not understand, stand under, or carry the burden.

But we must stop murdering
the good wishes
of the few who care enough
to step closer.

We must not swallow the burden
that was given to us by the unyielding,
blind universe
that could not or did not nurture us
so long ago.

The Caretaker

It's a steep climb. But stay vertical.
Replace each burly stone that rolls off the garden wall.
Chop onions and carrots for soup.
Sit beside your loved ones to count their daily pills.
Their faces are grateful and your face is dear.
This is all that's required of someone who cares,
and tries, and can be trusted.

But lately my need to embrace what has to be done
with faithful, hard-working hands flies out the window.
I shrug off obligation like a long coil of rope
you could use to hang me.
I spit my duties, bitter and bloody, into the wind,
until they soar off into the forgotten country,
where I'm neither kin nor kind.

When I was young I wanted to help in order to belong,
and needed to belong in order to survive.
But now when my heart is startled at being startled
by endless illness, pain, and suffering,
I try to remember not to put duty and worry
before peace and light and love.

Cold

She's cold and unresponsive. So is he.
I can't believe they were born that way.
The Ice Age must have crept upon them,
stiffened their backs, their faces, their eyes.
They turn away when life is too sad,
and rarely laugh or touch another's hand.
Life is better when they sip martinis
and you tell them they're smart and pretty.

They're cold for different reasons.
A broom weds a post, and gives birth to splinters.
Opposing flags stand out in high winds,
but neither country wins a single battle.
Maybe no one tells them how gifted they are,
how worthy of love. Who knows what might help?
Maybe nothing. Maybe they're just cold,
and I've decided it's not my job to warm them.

Soon they'll shatter, icicles collapsing
on brutal cement or stone, and then the sun
will urge them to leap into the waterfalls
of grief and pain that flow from every mountain—
the deep joy and hope buried in every rocky bed.
Hell, I can't remember what this poem is about
or what made me so angry, sad, and fearful,
now that I've traveled longer and farther
down my old, fond and faithful road.

Remarkable Me

When did remarkable me disappear?
I used to read Mark Twain and Edna Millay,
climb trees, ride wild horses, swim across rivers,
play the clumsy klutz and the ingenue.
Oh, the beauty and truth of being so young!

When did I forget to speak my true mind,
and toss out my mistakes with the trash?
When did I stop seeing music, jokes, or poems
in the gestures of every woman and man?
When did the burden of being me grow so great?

Some say I'm still remarkable me.
Maybe they're right. But doesn't the world demand
that we be unremarkable, safe in society's arms,
bathed in habit and compliance, lost in responsibilities
no one wants, but everyone praises?

I know more than I dare to say about futility,
illness, and death, and more than I need to know
about saying yes when I mean no.
I'm still remarkable when I wake and when I fall asleep,
and sometimes in-between, and the sooner I accept it,
the more true I'll be to myself when I die.

Yes, the sooner I embrace my heart and guts,
my ancient hands and feet,
the more life won't pass me by—
because I'm as remarkable as a pony or a peony,
a shadow or a sneeze. I'm as remarkable as you.
I am remarkably remarkable me.

When Women Speak Together

When women come to me with loving faces
to tell me I've written what they want to say,
and the first is a girl, pale from chemotherapy,
and the second cares for newborns
while she holds her dying husband's hand,
and the third, afloat in her sad, terrified flesh,
has powers she hasn't yet discovered,
and can only whisper her name...
I am swept back into my childhood.

Grandma gets off the bus, drops her gift-filled bags,
and cries, "There's my darling girl!"
Mother proudly reads my poems to her friends
though she never finished her poems
after my birth and the births of my siblings.
At ninety, she dreamed one night
that someone had stolen a book or a child from her,
she couldn't remember which.

So when women come and take my hand, I ask,
what is this perfect and mysterious message
we send each other, this vital, stabbing, healing,
peace-giving keepsake, this ebb and flow?
And why do I feel free to say, to those who listen,
"I'm lost at the moment, and half dead"?
Because in the very saying, in that secret joy,
I move into myself and toward another woman
who holds my hand, and says only and forever
her name, which is the same as mine.

Old Songs For New Weather

Now that I'm past my first and second prime
all the old songs are my favorites.
Their words and music rise from family picnics,
car rides down sultry summer streets,
high school basketball games and dances,
and those galloping college years
when we tramped the droning academic halls,
shouting and marching and swooning.

The songs return without my asking,
buried for years in my brain and bones,
stronger than the echoes of cadenced sermons
from graduations, marriages, or funerals.
No matter where I am, they follow me
just as I once followed them into some magical
landscape of the mind, lost in the feelings
born in every living note and phrase,
with a child's faith in their simple messages.

"I never will marry, I'll be no man's wife."
"Take my hand, I'm a stranger in paradise…"
"Don't think twice, it's all right."

63

What's Happened To My Brain?

I write *April* in October, and *6* instead of *26*.
I drop the *f* when I write *for* or *fun*,
lose track of who just phoned, and why,
and leave my purse on top of our car
or on our friendly garbage can.
My best pair of glasses are at the grocery,
and I've slept soundly on the second pair.
The faces of Amy Adams and Douglas Crowe—
no, *Russell* Crowe!—are burned into my brain,
but I can't always recall their names.
Meryl Streep! I've got her down pat.
And I know Shirley MacLaine and her brother
(what's his name?) are talented, too.
Take half of me and you've got an okay person,
but the rest of me is traveling downstream.
Where? There! That place I'm pointing to—
where willows bend over clear water,
bleeding the sweet smell of wild green,
and weeping with grief and gratitude.
I lie in our old gray boat beneath them
and hold out my arms to whatever I've loved
and never want to forget,
no matter what day, or what place,
and no matter what its name.

Dream About All The Relatives

Seemed like all the relatives came,
aunts, uncles, old Grandpa Rascal,
Grandma Moon, and sweet Nelly Brown,
seemed like all they wanted
was to see me, hear a kind word,
take my hand, gobble
a toddle of tea or a crumb of cake,
seemed like all I had to do
was let the dogs out,
one eager, one grumpy,
slinking into the light rain
falling on the shed, the worn grass,
the lost chicken, the sleeping cat,
seemed like I said
we could start a little fire,
a real one, with wood and flames,
and we did, and one cousin
I didn't remember ever meeting
couldn't talk because her jaw was healing,
and another cousin asked
how my baby was, and I said
fine, fine, though I hadn't spent
even one minute caring for her,
all bundled in white bunting,
because my other children did that,
though no one thought they would,
ah, but they were grown now,
strong and smart and capable,
though our house was really too small
for everyone, whoever some of them were,

65

but they claimed to be my kind of folk,
and they seemed so glad
to come inside to see me, after all.

The Girl With The Blue-Green Butterfly

After I wondered whether I had the courage to carry on,
one night as bright as day
I dreamed I flew to the small gray house on the sprawling yard
where I roamed as a child,
played in the bluebells, hid in the towering lilacs,
and where, later, we raised our children.

Yes here, one night as bright as day,
a torrent of flowers and fruits burst from the back door
and across the oak tree hills—
yards of lavender, gold, orange, and red, a chain,
a ribbon, a river of color—and who made this glory?
Who left this sweet gift behind?

A little girl came toward me, a slender water nymph,
a spirit of youth, promise, and joy.
She stretched out her hand to show me a blue-green butterfly
perched on her forefinger.
Her eyes glowed because this delicate insect trusted her,
and she looked at me just as trustingly.

And as we smiled, eye to eye, the butterfly flew—
looping, fluttering—from her finger onto mine,
touching me so slightly it was hardly there.

But I felt the wind from its wings when it flew
back to the little girl, then back to me—
to and fro, to and fro, it swam on air—
and we shared this moment as only a sharer can share,
and in that moment I trusted all the world.

IV

A WILD, GENTLE THING

Whatever it was I lost, whatever I wept for
Was a wild, gentle thing, the small dark eyes
Loving me in secret.
– James A. Wright, from "Milkweed"

Heartache

Her secret? It is every artist's secret.
Passion...an open secret, and perfectly safe.
 – Willa Cather

1

She can't speak—or maybe she *can*,
but words don't give voice to her anger, fear, and sorrow.

She lies down in tall grass beside the road
when her heart begins to rupture,

stands up to her waist in cold sea water
and debates slipping under, ready to leave forever,

paints pictures, writes in her journal, takes long walks,
and pays a wise healer to endlessly listen,

while this thing she calls her heart is almost broken,
like so many hearts on earth.

2

Her heart becomes her greatest enemy and her best friend—
her first and last responder,

telling her with every beat what she needs to say or do
though she doesn't always manage to say or do it.

At times her heart leaps up too sharply, too fervently,
as if it longs to leave its home,

as if it fears he may never find the tenderness or grit
to see who she is or what she feels—

or tell her what is true.

3

Her heart flails away from thoughts of murder
and becomes a victim—a remnant and reminder.

She's learned to hate herself
as if she were the source of the heartache

and she's learned to hate him
as if he were incapable of empathy, which he isn't.

Her straining, yearning heart sings of their future and their past,
and tells her she's tired of trying to force the two to meet.

But her heart is not a plant,
growing hopeful new tendrils every spring.

So, yes, she blames him. It gives her strength.
And it's the truth.

A Man Lies

A man lies when he wants another woman—
when he doesn't want another woman, but wants a secret friend—
when he sees the world with adolescent despair—
when he can't remember his mother or doesn't want to remember her,
or when he sees her in another woman's face—
or when he recalls his childhood in his dreams
and cries out in his sleep in the moonless night,
and his wife says, "Was it a bad dream?"
And he answers, "You know I never remember my dreams."

Stubborn

Stubborn as the day she was born, still sharing the same endless bed,
she lies beside him in all his giant complexity,
wandering uncharted seas, drowning in problems she cannot solve.

No hope in the looming, leaden sky all day, and no hope now
in the engulfing night, safe in one single waking moment
when she finally knows what she feels, because it's nightmare true.

But—who knows why he rides this fathomless subterranean wave
which rages out to the edge of the short time they have left?
Or why he couldn't share his secrets, when she trusted him?

Oh, let him take heart, even if she cannot. If she leaves,
he'll still have his prized past, born when he was too young to understand.
His dream wasn't real then, or now. But she was. And she is.

Trust

What is trust? she wonders.
Maybe it's when we dare to fly, like Peter Pan?
Or tumble down a rabbit hole with Alice?
Something amazing must be possible!

Can she hold trust in her hands?
Can she snuggle inside it to sleep?
Can she climb a cliff on a rope made of hope,
necessary lies, and cherished promises?

If he turns away, will trust re-enter her heart,
flow faithfully into her like a late summer night?
Trust may not last forever, but can it be re-imagined,
an old song that rises from the past as we face the future?

Yet she admits she doesn't trust anyone now.
She relies on her beating heart inside her ribs,
inside her skin, inside this day, beside the sea,
rocking in its bowl of sand and stone, a sacred place
from which she will not move, even when she dies.

Why? He promised he'd bury her here.
And he'd better, or he'll forever fear her ghost!

She Longs For Another Way To Love And Be Loved

She longs for another way to love, and be loved,
for plain words that rise from grief and peace, the enemies of fear.

She doesn't want to be cherished simply for her smiles or her songs
or for her fear of failing to love enough.

She wants what she thought they'd found years ago, something
he says they can have again, something she can no longer imagine.

He says he's always loved her, and will love her forever!

But this new emptiness stretches back, and back, to their beginnings,
reminding her of all that they have lost.

Maybe there was and is no love for her, and no god,
beyond the one inside her, smiling.

She wants love to flow from some other place,
a long slim ray of sun, sent just for her—to help her believe in death.

Nothing Pleases Her

Nothing pleases her when he enters the room
where she sits watching two snow geese on the water,
feeding, guarding each other, sailing into winter.

His beautiful eyes regard himself and his world,
but his lips do not welcome her.
His pressed pants and shirt are poised, respectable.

And that faithful, yearning young man she dreamed of,
lost her way for, found a new way for,
kept forever in her dreams—oh, that one is gone.

She can't see him even when she pretends he's there.
Instead, she embraces a slim thread, the precious truth,
where something's gone wrong, somewhere.

She didn't notice how he veered into a part of himself
he never wholly saw or shared—the assassin!—
fated to annihilate what he loved the most.

The Dream School

Panic rocks her bed at night with every heart beat
when she wakes and can't remember what she learned,
or why she was supposed to learn it,
in the dark, scary classroom of that grim dream school.
He says he loves her—
but what a strange way to show his love!

So in her next dream she drives with a kindly friend
toward the house where she grew up.
They find the winding road with some effort,
but the old house and garden are empty,
full of vague echoes of what she tended and loved,
or thought she'd tended and loved.

Nothing looks as she remembers it, except for one tall oak,
but even that seems wrong, misplaced, ill-timed.
She can't understand where she is or where she wants to be,
or even what bit of chaos she hopes to learn from next.
And she wonders who she is, in this savage new world—
with no teacher, no path, no ancient, well-kept home?

Does Her Fear Of Being Alone Keep Her With Him?

She lived alone for years, except some giddy lingering
with a boyfriend as loopy as a caterpillar smoking a hookah.

Now she wonders if she could bear to live by herself
after years of marriage, children, and too many breakfasts.

A fierce current inside her flowed out, out, into babies,
family, friends, and a man who's still with her, hand in hand.

But there's a worn, tired place inside her,
though she tries to send love with every greeting.

If she and he remain together, will the whole world of love,
and even the word *love* wing steadily toward them? Or away?

Or would it be better for her small blue-green planet
to roll on alone, healing, and ripe with promise?

Storm

Black rain clouds tower in the west,
while a yellow sun rises in the east.

Between darkness and light,
the sea takes on a spooky metallic sheen.

Wind-driven waves fly into flower shapes,
their petals meshing and un-meshing.

Lightning flashes, followed by thunder—
a growl, a pop, a shattered drum—

until, at last, rain pours down in a heavy tide
between her and a man she may never understand

despite their best efforts to swim together
in the pitiful raw language of feeling.

Nothing they say or do, raging or shining,
brings great change,

but this rain will take her where she needs to go,
into an awakening beyond her slim understanding.

This is the great dream and deep wish of water
and the truth of beginnings and endings.

This is how rain falls, without answers,
obliterating everything,
and how safe she feels in its powerful arms,

where there's nothing to do, no one to be—
where she breathes out the blackness of fate,
and swims free.

Strangle Him

How does she know she could strangle him?
She's done it in her dreams. Hands at his throat,
thumbs in the dents above his tender clavicles.

If he were a sexy rock star she'd still strangle him.
Yes, even if he were a town hall hero,
a man who "gives so much to his community."

If he were President, pastor, paratrooper, or paragon,
lowly sheepherder or cattle man, or *The man with the hoe*,
she would still, damn it, strangle him.

What if he were a transcendent trans-gender astronomer
with knowledge of every star, sun, or planet
and all their lovely, lonely moons? Well, too bad!

Or what if he were a hunchback, rowing her across
the River Styx amid the steady creak of oars
and the choking black smoke of danger?

She'd still have to strangle him, since so many
have struggled to make this crossing before her,
none strangers to the death or near-death of love.

And if the boat tips and she falls into the seductive,
wintry waters, infused with earth's last best tears,
she'll leap out and swim for shore—not alone, not lost.

"Let's make this trip together," she'll cry,
"and take our chances on the wild, raging waves
with our hands on our friendly, faithful hearts!"

So yes, she can and will strangle him
and put an end to this ageless wrestling match.
Before death—or after—she'll strangle him!

He Trembles

He trembles when he sees her in the sudden light of day,
hands cupped over his heart for protection,
anxious fingers dangling as she steps near
and they eye each other's eyes,
still soft and ripe with some remaining trust.

He's not sure if she still loves him.
Neither is she at this moment,
amidst the changes and turns of fortune.
Can she be with him now with her whole heart—
this man who is also a sweet child?

She wonders if he knows he's trembling?
She could try to comfort him,
but she may fail to find the strength,
since she's also a sweet child and a woman
who doesn't want to face him, or herself.

So she turns to the unblemished egg,
the tender crack of the shell over the smoking pan,
the raw surrender, the subtle hiss of yolk, fat, and flame,
and she waits for the rest of their life
to make itself known.

84

Fare Well

Two people meet, and glory erupts, along with truth and lies,
blunders and bliss, war and peace.

She works or plays, laughs or cries, stutters or sings—
and he does the same. And on they go,
with the usual mysterious uprisings in the wilderness,
knowing they will die, wondering how death will come—
beside a churning waterfall, in a dead-quiet hospital room,
or in their blessed sleep, half-awake to random fog and thunder.

And if she's lucky, she's not living with a stranger so strange
he can't see how much he means to her
or how much she means to him.
And so a great white silence descends, a snowy blizzard.
It's not indifference. She's cared too long to give up caring,
and her grief is a quiet soul keeping her alive.

She thinks of the chambers of her mind: white roots, green shoots,
scarlet petals, winged thoughts like milkweed parachutes in the wind,
and mushroom circles as large as a house—feelings!—
like clear waves that mesh with darker waves from every shore.
And with relief, she accepts that his presence in her life,
and hers in his, has become too much—absurd!

He needn't apologize for what he cannot be.
She needn't apologize for what she cannot be.
They needn't apologize for their goodbyes.

The Words They Choose

How can she know what he wants or who he is if he doesn't know?
He says one thing and does another, bends when he says he'll break
and breaks when he says he'll bend. Just like her.

Photos tell some of their story, half-lying about what they show,
but the true story changes shape and color before they can grasp it,
trying to survive the treacherous swamp of language.

Does every story depend on the words they choose? Yes.
Some words are sacred stones, whether fact or fiction,
though they rarely bow down before them.
They water their feelings down with sterile syllables
that speak of lost chances, old feuds, and havoc.

This is why she doesn't always believe him when he tells her
what he wants or who he is, any more than she believes herself.
So let them tell each other what they *will*. Let them do that. Now.

What She Learned About Love From Dreams

If every man you ever loved is in your dreams,
no wonder you're afraid of dying. So honor all your lovers
with a kiss, and ride the tides forevermore.

If a woman steals your seashell with the rainbow skin
and your lover won't look you in the eye—
march right in and take back your iridescent soul.

They had no right to swipe it, and lie about it, too.
And if you have nowhere to go where you feel loved,
listen to that old sea song, and you'll start to sing again.

You can push the heart right out of your chest
trying to get your lover back, but when you've driven him
half way home, he'll spit in your eye.

Be careful. You're older and wiser. The next time a tornado
races toward your home, you may save the one you love
and have no strength left to save yourself.

Remember that small green tree frog who slept all winter
in your begonia, and began croaking on the first day of spring?

He's not a dream.
Don't put him out until all danger of frost is over.

Intimacy

She doesn't want a boyfriend or a husband,
just a guy around the house on Tuesdays
who cooks and eats and sleeps with her,
a smart guy who wants her to read aloud
from her favorite books, and doesn't mind
when she cries or laughs, dances or dreams.
He's welcome to love anyone else,
cook for them, catch them on the fly,
just so he's with her on Tuesdays, forever.
She uses him to ease her path, so she won't
call him partner, significant other, or spouse.
He's more important than a constant lover,
and more reliable than family or friends.
And what will she give him in return?
Nothing. Not a thing.
Her simple birth and life and death.

Feeling Inadequate While Chewing On A Sausage...

...she realized she was never any good at blow jobs.

Or maybe she was fine, even respectable,
but she simply couldn't fathom how it worked.

If she admitted to herself that she was skilled,
life might become too stimulating.

And if she told others, they'd say she was bragging,
like a hotshot cheerleader whose team always wins.

In truth, maybe she wasn't good at any aspect
of making love or making love work.

Too hard to ghost out of her body and brain,
forget her nerves, worries, skinny arms and flat ass.

Not to mention his sturdy stance and lofty eyebrows
and her fear of failing to meet his expectations.

Maybe she grew up too fast in too many ways?
Well, so what if she looked twenty at fifteen?

She's lucky she's alive, still inhaling peace and joy
from the cottonwoods dancing silver in the wind—

safe in her body, surrounded by otherness and beauty—
at home at last in this world.

Her At Her Best

She doesn't want to know him better than he knows himself,
but her dreams won't stop seeking the fire
hidden beneath ashes that still breathe smoke.
That's how some dreams work.
You can follow their path into the tree tops,
into the stark blue sky, or over the sea,
when you know the one you seek is the one you love.

Her dreams tell her how protected he has to be,
and that he can't speak the language of a woman
who wants to put down her sword and shield
and feed him meat sizzling from the spit—
share it, blood, grease and all,
to remind him how vital it is to travel with someone you love,
two open-hearted wanderers, who don't keep secrets.

She tries to describe the hopeful feeling that rises in her heart
after the pain ebbs away—how, at times,
heat surfaces in her chest to warm and comfort her.
This is her answer to a killing blow,
and it's all she has now, whatever comes next.
Yes, it's her at her best, and it better be enough!
She sleeps well when this tender spirit eases her.

May it survive even death. Her death. Or his.

Starting Over

After months of feeling confused, angry, and afraid,
she asks herself at four in the morning,
"Where am I? What do I want? Who am I?"

At dawn her best self greets her, sad and certain, but true.
She's pregnant with gratitude,
flushed with a vital energy she can feel again.

She's a whole, wondrous being, just like him,
as welcome as anyone, weak and strong,
easily hurt and slow to mend, but buoyant.

This new feeling is a gift to herself.
She can be careful yet carefree, in danger yet safe—
no longer shattered, false to herself, or numb.

She trusts that she and he can be friends,
measured and graceful.

She's part of a small secret joy,
like a fragile mushroom in the first spring rain.

A New Home

Old age arrives like winter's shorter days,
frost-bitten but achingly lovely.
Leaves fall and winds rise,
whistling their death-song through windows and doors.

Old age is a careful walk down a sloping hill,
full of moments that whisper how fine it's been to know him,
and she loves him more than any other.

Now she seeks a magic home for them both,
where windows eye the blue-green distance.
An eternal place. Some might call it heaven.
But she calls it true earth.

She hears it call their names with a deep sigh,
flowing out, out—and then a full breath in.

To Be Known

1

To be known is rare. To see and be seen.
To feel those lucky embraces with the spiraling universe
when the wisest part of you feels the joy and pain,
the sweet affliction, of being with someone who knows you well,
even when you don't always welcome it.

2

How can we truly see and hear each other?
Even the most confident and supple hide something
from themselves, or from you and me.
Sometimes what is hidden wants to be known
even when we can't find the words or gestures,
and sometimes what we conceal happened so long ago
that memories can't carry all the truth.
So we stutter. We stumble. We understand, and then we don't.
We have to be reminded that we are as welcome
as we make each other, or ourselves.

3

Someone out there may move into your heart
and warm your skin as you warm theirs,
the way you swallow the sun's breath—
that light that embraces and shapes the spark inside you.
Knowing even one person can seem impossible.
But we're fond of each other. And we're worth it.
I want to know you. And I see you.
So it's your turn. You see me.

Surviving A Longtime Marriage

1

Let that lumpy old knapsack go
and those dull, pink, predictable petunias
and your perch on hard stone or kneeling on bone,
worrying which way the wind blows.
Who cares?

Let him, or her, or them, come toward you—
let them rant, rail, flail, or be frail;
let them sing or sigh, vomit and purge—
and blow on by.
Who cares?

Then let a bright, white, underwater stone,
shaped like a consummate egg,
catch your eye,
and greet you, meet you,
live beside you, anywhere.

Stay warm. Walk sweet.
Enter the cave. Welcome the rain.
Dare to hold hands with this one
who has walked with you
for more years than anyone else,
in boredom and suspense,
in wit and woe and wonder,
on grass, or ice, in sand, dust, or snow.

Do it for new time's sake.
But let go—let go—let go.

2

You're in the middle of a conversation
that began before you were born
and will end long after you die.

Your words echo in your secret-cave ears,
in your bee-hive chests, your lonely hearts,
your gentle breath just one strand
of a weaving which is forever unwoven,
then skillfully knit again.

Your voices flow back, toward your birth,
ocean into river, river into stream,
stream into underground sea—
all of this embraced by rock,
ancient, cracked, roiled, and smoldering—
only as solid as mother earth can be,

a music often unheard, impossibly far,
lost, yet never forgotten—
hoots, cries, and echoes with rugged, age-old notes—
something to let go of and hold close,
as you live and as you die.

About the Author

 Freya Manfred is a longtime Midwesterner who has lived on both coasts. She attended Macalester College and Stanford University, and has received a Radcliffe Grant and a National Endowment for the Arts Grant. Her sixth collection, *Swimming With A Hundred Year Old Snapping Turtle*, won the 2009 Midwest Booksellers Choice Award for Poetry, and her poems have appeared in over a hundred reviews and magazines and more than fifty anthologies. Her memoir, *Frederick Manfred: A Daughter Remembers*, was nominated for a Minnesota Book Award and an Iowa Historical Society Award. Her new memoir is *Raising Twins: A True Life Adventure*. She lives with her husband, screenwriter Thomas Pope in Stillwater, Minnesota. Their sons, visual artists Bly Pope and Rowan Pope have illustrated many of her books. Additional information is available on her website at www. freyamanfred.com

Made in the USA
Lexington, KY
09 September 2018